Last
Bus
to
Camden

Selected Poems

by Rocky Wilson

Cover Art & Design by William Butler
Edited by Sean Lynch
Interior Design by Erin Kelly

First Edition

Published February 13th, 2016, Camden's 188th birthday

Copyright © 2016 by Robert "Rocky" Wilson

All rights reserved. No part of this book may be reproduced by any means without expressed written permission from the publisher, editor, or author. Exceptions are made for brief excerpts in the cases of reviews or quotations.

Some of these poems were previously published in Painted Bride Quarterly, Friends Journal, and Whirlwind Magazine.

All inquiries should be addressed to:
Sean Lynch
P.O. Box 561
Camden, NJ 08101
or emailed requests to:
poetryandpoverty@gmail.com

Printed in the United States of America

∾

Acknowledgements

Poets Lamont Steptoe, Sean Lynch, and I sat outside The Victor's Pub in the refurbished RCA Building in Camden, enjoying the beautiful Indian summer day and the stunning view of the Philadelphia skyline. The wonder of the day for me lay not in what we were looking at, but in what Lamont and Sean were suggesting — that I gather my poems together into a book and get it published. I had been dreaming of something like this for more years than I'd like to admit, but never seemed to be able to take the steps necessary to bring the dream to fulfillment. If it weren't for Sean keeping me, who is so easily distracted, on task, there might never have been a book of collected poems.

Thank you so much, Sean, for all the editing, encouragement and enthusiasm that you brought to this project, with no thought of remuneration for yourself.

Thank you, Walt Whitman, my neighbor of 40 years, for paving the way, I should rather say for grassing the poetic pathway in Camden for me.

William Butler told me to close my eyes in his firehouse studio, then said, "Open them." I saw the beautiful cover he made, and my eyes got wet. The cover itself became its own beautiful poem, inviting others to enter my world.

Thank you Angela Boatright-Spencer for taking a look at the manuscript and catching mistakes that Sean and I missed.

I would like to thank my grandmothers who kept the old ways and the "old time religion" alive for me. My maternal grandmother, Molly "Nano" Robinson, rode a bike until she was 65 and my Dad's mom was the epitome of her name, Grace.

Thank you Dad for showing me the poetry of doing and for the Christmas roses you took every year to Mrs. G, whose son, your best friend, was killed in World War II.

I wish to thank Cousin Jo for believing in me and for gathering the poems and pictures of our families and making it so much easier for me to put things together. I am even writing this on a travel drive that Jo gave me.

My sister, Sandy, has helped keep the memories of our growing up so alive for me.

Thank you Peter Murphy and all the writing teachers I have had all the way back to Mrs. Clevenger who gave me a B- on my first poem in Junior High calling it "anti-climactic."

Thanks to my little brother, who didn't make it, but who I once felt kick in Momma's belly on the beach in Ocean City.

And thanks to all my great friends and everyone who helped kick start this book. To any who wished me well or thought a positive thought thank you too.

And above all thanks to my mother,
who helped me see flowers in Camden.

TABLE OF CONTENTS

Editor's Introduction: I

Ryokan: V

Short Cuts: 1

Local Anthem: 3

Box Score: 4

Food and Fuel: 5

Namesong: 7

The Wisdom of Owls: 9

Hammock Moon: 11

The R5: 12

Fall Haiku: 14

Bloodline: 15

Hang Time: 17

Beside the Delaware on Emily Dickinson's Birthday: 19

Big Dipper: 21

It Was Like Hitch-hiking: 22

Candlemas: 24

Winter Haiku: 25

Stopwatch: 26

Could it Have Been the Ginkgo Biloba?: 28

Haiku: 30

Christian Science: 31

Horse Whispers: 33

Equinox: 35

Spring Haiku: 37

Rita, My Mother Saw Daffodils: 38

Revival: 39

Opera Comes to Camden: 41

Buddha Orders the Lunch Special: 43

A Chance: 44

Haiku: 45

Touching Home: 46

Senryu: 47

Stepping: 48

Still Counting: 50

Stellwagen: 51

She Left for Sierra Leone: 53

Summer Haiku: 55

Code Orange: 56

On the Bus to Cape May: 57

Broken Arms: 58

Put Down Dogs: 59

Stanley's Picture: 61

Peace, Brother: 63

Dear Mom,: 65

Surrender: 67

Ship Bottom: 70

Tripping: 71

There are no Movie Houses Left in Camden: 72

Editor's Introduction

The bus ride to Camden from the JFK Airport felt longer than I had expected. Post-industrial New Jersey's passing scenery was dreary in contrast to the rolling green pastures of western Ireland that I'd grown used to in the past week. I owed a classmate a couple hundred Euros borrowed out of desperation, and so immediately headed to an ATM as soon as we arrived at the Rutgers campus, paying him back with even more borrowed money from my hard-strapped working-class parents.

I should have been happy — I'd just returned from the trip of my dreams, but the lack of cash from my minimum wage job and impending student loans compounded with the excessive heat, even for early June. I was a sweaty mess. My mindset was in self-centered, pissed off at the world mode. And yet my mood began to clear as we stepped off the bus, because in the distance I spotted a bronze, glowing figure atop a bicycle, calling out in a high pitched voice to pedestrians while waving around a monkey puppet. I knowingly smiled, but my creditor-companion bore a look of mild concern.

While we unloaded our suitcases the disheveled person dismounted his mountain bike and approached us. This man was darkly tanned with shining gray hair, wearing a black tank top, shorts, and sandals. His bike basket was filled with fruit and miscellaneous items. He was gazing at the Philadelphia skyline behind us.
"Rocky!"
"Sean! I thought you were in Ireland!"
We hugged each other.
"Just got back. You're so tan."
"I was in Atlantic City. Where's my post card you promised?"

I apologized to Rocky for not being able to send it due to something called a "Bank Holiday," then handed him a card that displayed an aerial view of the Aran Islands.
"It's beautiful. Thank you so much Sean."

I

I almost didn't recognize him without one of his signature rainbow tie-dye shirts. We talked briefly about the Aran Islands and western Ireland, as he'd been there a few years earlier for a poetry festival. He visited the cottage on Inishmaan where John Synge lived. I asked him when his next Pizza and Poetry reading was taking place (the date changes every month, a small reflection of Rocky's mercurial personality). Then I told him we'd have to meet for a beer at The Victor, but that I had something to take care of at the moment with my friend. Rocky said hello and introduced himself, as well as Bongo, his monkey puppet, then they both took off toward the Delaware River.

My friend was baffled.
"Was that a hobo?"
"No. He's a poet."
"Oh…"

Serendipity caused Rocky to welcome me back home, helping me smile in a moment I needed it most. Without that simple greeting I'd have remained depressed. Instead of seeing flowers and grass, I would have stared at abandoned buildings and broken asphalt. Rocky lives one block away from where we had stood, on Penn Street in Camden. His home is a beautiful three story brick row-house built nearly a century ago. He acquired it for only a dollar from a friend turned monk journeying to Italy on a permanent stay. When Rocky moved in his welcome to the neighborhood present was a brick through the window.

My more fortunate welcome home from Ireland wasn't the only time that I'd introduce Rocky to someone and they thought that he was an eccentric homeless person. He's oblivious to so-called social norms. This is because Rocky Wilson is the epitome of what it truly means to be anti-establishment, and although he grew up in comfortable Haddonfield, he's far from a bourgeois poser. In the 70's, Rocky felt the need to return to the decaying city of his birth,

Camden, not to evangelize, but simply because the rent was cheap. Unpretentiously he would begin to spread enlightenment to the wounded city. And to Rocky that involves both poetry and puppetry. "The puppet man" some call him, he prefers to declare himself the Puppet Laureate of Camden. Why not? Rocky Wilson is an outsider who makes a real difference in America's most infamous city, along with priest and poet, Father Michael Doyle. However, Rocky isn't a grassroots activist; he manages to stay above the political fray. He's much more than that. He lives the pure life that aspiring beatniks could only wish to lead; he is the grass, one blade
among many.

    Rocky brings joy to the hearts of strangers, especially children. As a substitute teacher in Camden, Rocky has built relationships with residents of the city that have endured for decades. It seems like every time I walk down Cooper Street with him a local calls out "Mr. Rocky! Where's Bongo?" Rocky replies with heart-warming sincerity, a virtue present throughout his poetry
as well.

    At first glance Rocky Wilson's poems could be dismissed as confessional or romantic — the former being over-killed by the beat poets of the last century, the latter in the century before that and since. Those influences can still be seen in these pages, although a close reading will reveal myriad collages with an awareness of what has preceded it, but with a subtlety that is neither unnecessarily referential nor deliberately obfuscating. Rocky illuminates the life-giving poet-gardener aura free of irony in contrast to the literary cynicism prevalent today that's doomed to cyclical self-destruction.

    The status quo has largely been stagnant for decades. In this age ruled by the academia, when too many poets are mired in elitist obscurities, the insincere become touted as the avant-garde of North American poetry. Rocky Wilson brings us back to our poetic roots in the democratic spirit of Walt Whitman, which may seem trite to some, but it's necessary in our fragmented and bewildered society. This poet proves that what's needed isn't art reflecting more confusion, but art that cures confusion. He does this when he recognizes subconscious pain stemming from a lost baby brother, when he bears witness to natural beauty surviving among urban ruins, when he meditates on the potentiality of love, when he observes camaraderie between whales, and in many more ways.

    These poems may seem like stories at times, prosaic, narrative driven, conclusive. That's what makes this book touching and original and even potentially invaluable to those exhausted with the current state of literature. This is exactly what America needs. Poems that flow like seasons. Meaningful words. Poetry that combats materialism and death — poetry motivated by peace, and daringly enough, the human spirit.

- Sean Lynch

"Who says my poems are poems?
My poems are not poems.
After you know my poems are not poems,
then we can begin to discuss poetry."
—Ryokan

SHORT CUTS

My father had special scissors
with rounded ends
for cutting nose hairs.
To me, living in a tree house
in the Berkeley hills in 1969,
Dad's fastidiousness was just part
of his strange dance to the far right.
In a three piece suit, fedora and solid red tie
my father traveled the hills of Pennsylvania
selling his dyestuffs,
while I, in tie-dye,
traveled the hills around San Francisco Bay
watching red-tailed hawks soar
above pages of my poetry.

This autumn, back east, in the city of my birth,
I take my father's small scissors
from the travel kit I inherited and put it to use.
Water swirls into the porcelain sink
and the little black hairs disappear.
I rinse my face and get a vision of Dad
hovering over huge silver vats
mixing colors that have no names,
colors that no one has ever seen before.
The Grateful Dead is playing and Jerry Garcia,
who is wearing a hairnet,
tells my father to add more vermilion.

It's funny at first, but when I see my father's blue eyes
looking back at me from the mirror,

my smile begins to take on water
until I am drowning in the number of years we knew
and didn't know each other at all.

Out my bathroom window in the yellow mulberry
sits Robin, our pale blue family parakeet from the 50's.
He holds a tiny olive branch in his beak.
When I lift the sash, I can hear the wind.
Somewhere people are saying
this is the most colorful autumn
they can remember.

LOCAL ANTHEM

I live in Camden,
not exactly what people have in mind
when they sing "Home of the brave
and land of the free."
But my angels have gotten me out
of some squeezes.
The crack-head's knife missed my lung
by half-an-inch.

A young girl once pleaded and pushed me
off a mean street in Parkside.
I had been her substitute teacher
and she called me "bad"
which meant I was "good."
Then this gang saw me jogging
over by Camden High
and was ready to bust me up
when they saw a monkey on my hand
and realized, "Hey, this dude
is the Puppet Man."

What saves our lives:
a 6th grade girl,
a little cloth monkey,
a dull knife,
an angel's wings
brushing through
the ghetto night.

BOX SCORE

Last night at the dance improv workshop
I touched my partner's slender wrist
and my fingers slipped
onto the deeper skin
stretched over the hollow boned frame
of this singing world.
At the end she placed my hand
on my own heart
and, then, we turned away
like lovers uncoupling.

The next morning I let the sports section
fall to the floor and find the fat blue
"Norton Anthology of American Poetry."
There it is, "A Blessing," by James Wright.
with the line describing the ear of a pony
"…delicate as the skin over a girl's wrist."

My blue eyes examine the thin blue lines
of my own wrists while she awakens slowly in Mt. Airy.
I stretch my pink fingers across the rivers between us,
gently rub the sleep from her eyes and whisper words,
from an almost forgotten English class,
words that she sends back
bearing dark red promises,
like a late September
second coming
of raspberries.

FOOD AND FUEL

Laura is late but doesn't show it.
She strolls down Cherry Street smiling like the October sun.
Then I see why. She is wearing wings,
wings she reluctantly takes off
to get into the car
"I've got cheese, apples and seduction bread," Laura says,
and I add laughter and a bottle of red wine to the list.
We cross the sparkling Delaware,
hit 676 and fly through Camden,
past the steeples and boarded up buildings.

I don't touch the brake until the Frank Farley Rest Stop
along the Atlantic City Expressway.
The smell of apple cider doughnuts greets us
and I buy a half-dozen, while Laura heads for the bathroom.
My old Beamer seems to need more rest
because when I turn the key it balks.
"Oh, well," Laura says and reaches for the wings.

The next thing I see is Isadora Duncan in bare feet
prancing around a young maple.
I cannot believe I know this dark haired, winged beauty
who turns the rest stop into anything but.
Laura gives the flagpole her elbow
and spins around old glory,
then she is up on the picnic table,
then down in the grass, like she, not Whitman
had written the book.
A woman buys a can of soda but doesn't open it.
A man puts down his hamburger.
Even a small black poodle stops sniffing a bush,
to watch Laura.

A few more twirls, a small leap, a burst of light
and then a slow, graceful end.
A little girl tells Laura how much she liked the dance.
Laura floats back to the car, which starts right up.
"See," says Laura.
And I do see.

NAMESONG

Just when the maples
are adding shades of color
to match the wildfire of her hair,
Nancy has invited me up to her lake house.
It is such a pleasure to trade the crazy Friday traffic
for the patterns of wild geese.
The deer Nancy is so used to seeing
are still a wonderful surprise to my Center City eyes.
I stop the old BMW beside a cut cornfield,
and a half-dozen does wave good bye
with the white hankies of their tails

From Nancy's driveway,
the wind whipped lake seems about to rise
and extinguish the bowl of burning autumn hills,
but by the time Nancy and I finish cups of Jasmine tea
the wind is doing a much slower dance
and we slide the canoe into the water.

Half-way across Lake Galena
Nancy's voice adds
"The Colors of the Wind"
to the song of our paddles.
"I did my first solo at a music workshop last weekend,"
she says, turning her head towards the splash of a carp.
"There was a couple there from Ohio
who sang song after song
for their lost daughter."
I surprise myself when I tell Nancy
about a baby brother who choked on the cord
and went into the ground without a song or a name.

"Once at dinner, Dad left the table
and my little sister and I heard sobs
coming from the living room.
'Your father wanted another son,' Mom told me."
Nancy, who has turned her head to look at me, winces.
"After that my brother was never mentioned again."

Later, near the dock,
the canoe frightens a great blue heron
that with a series of croaking sounds
flies majestically across the lake.
"How could it look so graceful" Nancy laughs,
"and sound like a dying frog."
I think of my brother,
as the heron disappears
into the colorful hills—
a stork returning the baby
to sender.

THE WISDOM OF OWLS

The perfect line came over the ridge
with the just beginning to wane moon.
I woke in the moose quilt bed
with ten or so words that, I felt sure
would become my owl totem and lead me
on silent wings
to a wonderful poem.

No need to write the line down.
No way I could forget it.
But when the sun finally broke the moon's hold,
Poof!
I imagine all these killer first lines,
these dazzlers,
these hook-line-and-depth-charge lines
lost in a flimsy red-eyed dreamland,
but, perhaps, not totally gone,
perhaps, able to be border-collied
into a green pasture somewhere
with someone like Rumi
to tend them—
free range lines,
organic, grain-fed.

No, you cannot buy these lines
or ever study hard enough
to produce them yourself.
You can just let your own owl loose
on the moon swept edges of the dark
and hope for the best.
And, maybe, decades later you will
eschew morphine on your going Home bed

and that lost line will fly through the window
of the hospice and AHA you
with the brilliance of the aurora borealis.
In fact, all that you have lost
may well return on snowy wings
to build a star studded staircase
for the climb up past
the raised eyebrow of the moon
to the house of light and song
that Rumi has prepared for you.

HAMMOCK MOON

The crescent moon
tired from too many late nights
sleeps in the hammock left by the lake.
The understanding snow covers her
and that's where the sun finds her
in the surprise wonder
of a white October morning.

THE R5

Maybe I'm sitting where you sat
early this morning on your way
to teach language arts in Paoli,
the remnants of your Olay scent
overpowered by commuter's coffee.
I'm taking the train the other way
to a dance rehearsal in Doylestown
where three years ago
we hiked through the disappearing green
of Peace Valley Park.

Remember the darkening sky,
the watering hole and tall grasses,
where two blond-haired, blue-eyed deer
laid themselves down.
As tongues searched for Indian Summer salt,
a slow, rhythmic rock of bodies
gathered blind speed
faster than light we rode the glory train
arrived before we left
as the clouds cracked
and water poured down
doused the sparks flying
from the flint and steel
of our hips
and kept the dry grasses
from turning to flame.

We streamed through the open veins
of the flooding earth
washed finally onto the bank
near the stone bridge.

Laughter bounded after us
when we leapt as one
over the chain across the fire road.

Back at the car a stranger
snapped a photo
that we could look at years later,
"Here, this is us, wet and in love."
Your wide and beautiful eyes
the last trace of deer left
for the camera.

We have separate photo albums now,
but, still, a trail connects us
like the glowing gossamer
lines left by snails
in your garden
the first night
we met.

FALL HAIKU

Missing its color,
the bare maple reaches
for my rainbow cap.

Shutting off
the porch light — the moon
stays on

Veteran's Day,
my prayer flags frayed
to almost nothing.

BLOODLINE

When I screamed so loud Momma froze,
Grandmom came and sucked the poison
out of the rusty nail hole.
We buried her in the lavender dress
my sister made
with the crescent moon pin
my father bought for her
with paper and lawn money
during the depression.

Once, like Abraham,
she raised the sharp edge of that moon
over my father.

It was like this.
She voted for Wilson
who promised to end all wars
and that was her last Democrat.
When my father was drafted
Grandmom prayed that if it came down to it,
his life be taken first.
She didn't want him to live
with another man's life
on his conscience.
Two days before he was to land
on Normandy Beach
my father got the measles.

Today I run my fingers over the names
of people killed in Vietnam.

I find my friend's name
and pieces of my grandfather's name,
my father's name and my own.
Then I take a curved bone
from the lavender sky
and begin sewing
these names together.

HANG TIME

I try to tackle my little brother
but he's fast and slippery,
as quick as I have him
he's gone again,
the Galloping Ghost.
His birthday's on Thanksgiving this year,
with all the big turkey games.
But his own holiday comes in October,
still in the heart of football season,
a day of remembrance
for those lost at birth.
There must be others, then,
more than enough for two teams
to play out those first few seconds
again and again,
call the same plays over and over,
"If only the cord hadn't...."
"I wish the doctor had...."
Snap count,
the number of tears
my father choked back
when he left the dinner table.

Under the Christmas tree
there's a tiny black and red letter sweater
with an "O"
a zero, the time he got to play.
Not enough quarters
to get a real Haddonfield High "H."
I got my 16 quarters
hiking on all those punts
our lousy team had to make.

They put "Robert," not Rocky,
on my award certificate.
His death certificate says "Babe Wilson,"
a great athletic name
male or female.
I felt you kick just once
in Momma's big belly on the beach
in Ocean City.

"Yo, Babe, get way back,
I'll hike you one!
Give it a good high kick,
plenty of hang-time,
pin 'em deep in their own territory.
Don't worry, I'll keep track of your quarters
and you, way up in the sky box,
can keep track of mine."

BESIDE THE DELAWARE ON EMILY DICKINSON'S BIRTHDAY

Miles from the nearest maple,
I see a bright red leaf that turns out to be a cloth flower.
A sea gull lands under the Ben Franklin Bridge
as a high speed train rumbles over it.
To the south, in Gloucester, is the Walt Whitman
and in between bridges, Walt, himself,
sings a happy Song of Herself to Emily.
The river carries the song all the way to the water gap
and then mockingbirds in parkas continue with it north
to Amherst where they deliver it to Emily
whom is out in the garden already planning for spring.

Last night's fierce wind, snuffed out by someone kind,
has left the river calm, even at high tide.
There's an old schooner docked in Philadelphia,
beside newer Navy ships here for the big game with Army.

"There is nothing like a frigate
To take us lands away
Nor any coursers like a page
Of prancing poetry…"
Emily sings back to Walt.
They don't need the river or mockingbirds any longer.

A man is sleeping on a river bench
covered by a Spiderman sleeping bag.
He is dreaming of super powers
and a glass of milk.
A fire and rescue boat sits alone
in the small Camden harbor,
it being so far past Labor Day.

And yet you, Emily, are still wearing white.
Who cares if it's almost winter?
Your dress, I read, has been hermetically sealed
in the secret vaults of Amherst College.
Late at night professors of English Lit
hold their collective breath
as they fondle the white lace.
The dress shown at your house
is a beautiful fake,
stitched at great expense
by the Smithsonian seamstress.

Who is the original being saved for?
By the year 3,000 will there be anyone left
who even remembers what poetry is?

How does Sunday look, Emily?
Walt and I will be up for the weekend.
Not to worry, we can order pizza
at the new parlor down the road
from your house.

If you're not up to seeing us
you can lower a basket of gingerbread down
from your bedroom window
like you do for the children.
Walt and I would be happy with the crumbs,
happy to just get a glimpse of you
in your own perfect white at the window,
to set us off on the right course
for the coming of winter.

BIG DIPPER

First ice late December,
thin layers lifted carefully off puddles
smashed in the street like glass.
Only once-in-a-while ice now
but back before the war
thick Minnesota ice
blown over the Great Lakes
across Indiana, Ohio, the Alleghenies
to Hoppies Pond, New Jersey.

"Could drive a car on that ice," Uncle Jay said,
his big hands showing how thick it was,
"build fires on it." Told how
golden carp with nothing left to eat
rose to the surface and froze there,
preserved till spring.
"Skated right over 'em
their big eyes staring up at the stars."

An old Model-T did go through once.
Uncle Jay got it out two years later
when the dam broke, fixed it up
drove all the way to Key West
and won the bet.
Came home with new jokes,
got married,
joined the army,
fought the Japanese in the jungle heat.
Came back with jokes he couldn't tell,
a red kimono for Aunt Jane
and a huge desire for ice.

IT WAS LIKE HITCH-HIKING

Only Blondie picks me up in church
between the split peace soup and Caesar salad.
We cross state lines like Bonnie and Clyde
killing with a monkey puppet named Bongo
who pays all the tolls with banana chips
and "Happy New Years!"

Blondie is a demon for speed
and somewhere past Flemington,
I imagine the Grand Prix doing a feathered roll
that catapults us into the ether.
We share the sky with turkey vultures
who thank Blondie for all the road kill.

Back on the highway
we stop at a house just past Great Adventure
where Blondie takes little vials of water
from the Atlantic and Pacific
out of a cedar chest.
My outstretched palms hold oceans
that turn my heart into Illinois. Abe Lincoln's sorrow
bows to his laughter and their dance
curls through us like the ferned ends of lightning
with nothing to strike.

Blondie gives me a piece of the Badlands to take home.
Time becomes the kiss of insects on the windshield.

She drops me off on the western edge of New Jersey
with the words, "Have you ever seen the full moon
surf along the edges of waves?"

The second week of January
I am at the tip of Jersey's cape
watching a sea dazzled by the moonlight.
The steady drum of surf
hypnotizes what rationality is left
and I step naked out of a little pool of clothes
into the bigger pool before me.
A thousand needles tattoo ice
into my veins and every frantic utterance
begins with the word, Holy.
Shivering my way back
in damp clothes to the Grand Hotel's hot tub
I see my picture
stuck to a "Lifeguards Off Duty" sign,
only I am young, dark haired
and riding a skateboard.

CANDLEMAS

His alarm set, the groundhog sleeps.
It wouldn't do to be late
for his one-day-a-year job.
It's his few minutes of fame.
Sun or clouds—shall he
run back to the burrow
or shall he dance?
Whatever he does, we're halfway
between the winter solstice
and the vernal equinox.
February 2nd
Celtic Spring.
You have heels, lads and lassies,
become foals or fools
and kick them up.
The light slants to the north,
winter, despite reports to the contrary,
is on the run.
A faint blush returns
to Walt Whitman's cheek
as the daffodil bulbs begin
to dream.

WINTER HAIKU

I walk in deep snow
and think of my dead father—
mist on the mountains.

A circle in the snow
where the trashcan was,
Valentine moon.

I sled past graves
as snow fills the names
etched in stone.

STOPWATCH

The Imax movie on whales wasn't cheap,
but Laura just looked down at her rainbow leg warmers
so I broke a twenty for both of us.
While the short feature took me flying over
Independence Hall, Old City, and the
Ben Franklin Bridge, Laura took off her
blue and white whale scarf and said,
"look at this"
"Shhhh."
I was stuck in the body of a soaring bird
and the taboo of talking in a movie.
The expression on her beautiful face
forced me to land on the parkway
between the flags of Uganda and Uruguay.

The breaching saved us.
A blue whale is the height of a 9 story building
and a small child could swim through its veins.
A humpback's song can go on for 30 minutes.
There was not enough breath left
to be upset with each other.

When I tried to admire Laura's scarf after the movie
the tiny blue whales dove quickly under her green coat.
I did get a look at her favorite t-shirt,
"Give Peace a Dance"
Laura's watch said 11:11, that's what it always said.
Neither of us wanted to trade the South Seas
for Philadelphia in February.

Hot chocolate sounded good but who would pay?
Not me again, she wasn't even my girlfriend.
We parted near Logan Fountain,
where the statues were snowed in,
she going west toward her apartment,
I east, toward mine.

Now Laura's watch sits upstairs in my drawer.
If there had been a wishbone in the ashes
we placed in the sea,
I would have asked the waves for more time,
for one more chance to say,
"Two hot chocolates, please,
with whipped cream,"
for one more chance to touch the whales
that swam so delicately
around Laura's neck.

COULD IT HAVE BEEN THE GINKGO BILOBA?

The colors missing
from the foggy February days along the Delaware
had started to appear brilliantly in my dreams.
Sometimes the full moon triggered a certain vividness
but according to the paper the moon was just a smile.
Johnny, from our old commune in Vermont,
was smiling too, when he went flying by my house.
He had been 19 on the farm, and smoked a lot of pot,
but he was the one who always drove the horses
up to the sugar bush to collect the sap. I trusted him,
so I stepped out the second floor window
like I was walking out the front door.
We flew together down Penn Street,
our whole bodies breathing in city lights,
and the dark air.
Around the corner Ernie Gowen,
the fullback from my high school team, appeared
and started grabbing at my ankles.
He wanted what we had but my scolding
turned him into a grunt.
Johnny had a beautiful sister, Rebecca,
who I wished had been there.
They both looked like they could have risen
out of a William Blake watercolor.
Where are they now?

And where are Turtle, Polly, Martha, Mary, and David X
the ones who collected
bucket after bucket from the dripping trees?
Where is Lucy, who, while supper cooked,
sat on a sap bucket and turned wool into winter warmth?
Where is Robert, who hearing the frogs peep
during the last run of sap, named the farm, Frog Run?
Where are they all?
Do they star in each other's dreams?
Do they, on long winter nights,
collect the singing buckets
and distill the sap
into sweet flight?

HAIKU

By dusk the man
has painted the steeple
and half the moon.

Tattered black
plastic caught on branch—
more crow than crow.

The white cat
brings all the light up
out of the basement.

CHRISTIAN SCIENCE

"He's guaranteed to talk,"
the St. Petersburg birdman promised
my grandmother, who had just lost her husband of 40 years.
On the train and back home
she never stopped the pretty boys
but the gift of talk wasn't in the green and yellow parakeet.
Every night, though,
after John Facenda signed off his newscast
Petey would give her a peck on the lip.

Holding her black handbag like a vise on the bus to Philly,
Gram saw the skid-row drunks teetering down Vine Street
and couldn't believe God took Pop
instead of one of the good-for-nothings.
Soon she, who loved to say,
"It's time to climb the wooden hill,"
had arthritis so bad she couldn't even
crawl up the stairs to bed.

The oven made Gram an offer,
no match, just turn on the gas
and it would be like going to sleep,
but she was afraid someone might come in
smoking a cigarette
and unwillingly go with her. And, also, there was Petey.
The Christian Science Church sent over tuna casseroles
and a healer, who pointed out Gram's wrong thinking.

She had built a tower
of resentment
higher than Babel.

The healer and my grandmother
found a common language
and gradually the winos became people
and the Mt. Everest of steps
became a wooden hill again.
And Petey's whistle, she was sure,
sounded more and more
like my grandfather's
with every passing day.

HORSE WHISPERS

I am from the initialed hearts, carved so long ago, into the elephant skin of the beech tree. I am from the blooming mountain laurel. I am from the ancient modern dance their smooth branches do in the gracious shade. I am from the zigzag afternoon light illuminating the rough bark of the tallest oak. I am from the outlandish burl on a nearby relative of that oak. I am from the cancer that...

I am from the cement slab that holds my cousin's memorial bench. I am from the mallard waddling toward the water. I am from the far off yowling of the children on the Tatem School playground. I am from the sound of my own childhood crying at that same school, where my mother left me to learn from the teacher who taught her. I am from the alphabet song that helped me identify letters like the ones on the plaque at my feet.

'In Loving Memory of my husband
William Jay Giesecke'

I am from Bill and me, four years ago, riding the waves on boogie boards down in Stone Harbor. I am from the cans of Coors Light beer we finished off in the parking lot of the church before going to visit my Mormon sister. I am from what Bill told me there beside the stone church,

"at 13, I had to give my mom shots of morphine to keep the pain from strangling her."

And how a friend of his brought a horse by the house for Aunt Jane to see, but she was too weak to get up off the couch. I am from the three words she whispered to Bill,
"bring him in."

I am from the living room where the gentle muzzle of the horse touched my aunt's thin cheek. I am from the tears Uncle Jay wouldn't let any of the four boys shed at the funeral.

I am from these woods where Bill and I, in cowboy hats, once shot each other with cap guns. I am from the dream Bill's daughter had after he died, of Aunt Jane with her dark hair flowing behind her riding bareback to meet him in a field of wild poppies.

I am from my own tears and the brittle circle of now wet leaves at my feet. I am from the tender green that will soon come up through all this mottled brown.

EQUINOX

It is the exact moment of spring,
recorded by the ranger's watch
and punctuated by gongs
of the big bell
outside the nature center.
A buck,
like some graceful prize-fighter,
bursts out of the brush
on the far side of the lake
and bounds across the ice.
His winter-light body
makes it to the lake's center
before the ice
gives way to spring
and the deer plunges
into the frigid water.
Now there is a second deer
running up the softening
backbone of winter.
It will surely pull up short
on the safe ice
and take the long way around.
But the second deer
is not backing off.
It is racing across the same break-
neck ice as the first deer,
whose head is visible now,
whose legs are fighting their way
through the freezing water.
Just as the lead deer
is clambering onto stronger ice
the second deer is swallowed up.

Then there is a third deer running
and a fourth and fifth,
wild hooves beating the grey sky of ice
back to a life-giving blue.
Deer in ancient, forgotten numbers,
not satisfied with shrieks and bells,
carrying spring across the blueing heavens
in their raw courage,
sick-of-winter hearts.
Carrying the high holy day
and hour and minute
of spring
across Lake Galena,
across Peace Valley Park.
No more dry grass
buried under a foot
of hard snow.
No more tough bark.
No more tasteless twigs
and deadwood.
Winter is gone, broken,
and the deer,
still breathing hard,
gather on the other side,
near the big willow,
shake themselves like dogs
but not like dogs,
shake the last cold drops
of winter
into the grasses
of spring.

SPRING HAIKU

After the rain
spring sun on pine needles,
warmth on my bald spot.

The mallard
at lake's center acts
like a loon.

Long after the eggs
could possibly hatch
the goose still sits.

RITA, MY MOTHER SAW DAFFODILS

Rita, I remember our conversation,
old wood begins to sprout leaves,
trees grow where desks stand,
the history of the people
carved into them.

Meanwhile, Jackson Pollock's mom
continues to mess up her apron
with all kinds of colorful food,
hoping the grandchildren
will catch the hint Jackson did
and paint.

It was so many tomatoes
and beets and mustard squeezes ago.
It's hard to remember
all the debts we owe.

My mother saw daffodils.
I was cleaning her windows
and dropped yellow paper towels
onto the grass.
She didn't see a messed-up yard,
she saw daffodils.

REVIVAL

(Walt Whitman died on March 26, 1892 and
Robert Frost was born on March 26, 1874)

"If you miss it this time
your next chance comes
in 16,000 years."
Last night over Camden
the comet Hyakutake
was a drop of spilled milk
along the handle
of the Big Dipper.

Today we'll spill wine
onto Whitman's grave,
sing "Happy Death Day!"
and then gather around his bed
in that little house on Mickle Street.
If we're lucky, the spirits
will help us trace
the Good Gray Poet's last breath
down to the river he loved.
Help us feel the feather of warmth
riding on a dark gust
of cold spring air.

North, the breath will turn,
like an ancient bearded salmon,
tired of salt and clamshells, swimming up river
toward the singing mountains of its birth
and death.

A great gale catches
the poet's last breath
and it arrives in an old
New Hampshire farmhouse
just in time for the party.
"I sing myself and celebrate myself,"
the breath whispers to the young poet,
"for every atom belonging to me
as well belongs to you."
And the breath is gone
pulled down deep inside
as the room darkens.

Then, roaring up out of him,
bellowing, blowing over sweet cake,
melting wax and eighteen
dancing flames,
this last great breath,
rising now with the heat,
becomes a comet itself
and charges off toward the sun.
There is another great suck of air
and Frost himself begins a wild arcing leap
into the starry New England sky.

OPERA COMES TO CAMDEN

The man of so many words left us with only two,
"Shift, Warry," Whitman said to his male nurse,
wanting to be turned in his bed on a rainy March night.

Was it for Walt Whitman you came north, Patricia,
up from the long poetic arm of Neruda's Chile,
followed by the songs of a thousand migrating birds?

In 1992, with only a spotted hawk for company,
I recited the end of "Song of Myself"
for the 100th anniversary of Whitman's death.
The audience, with only a little prompting,
sang "Happy Death Day."

You died on that same stage, Patricia,
as Gilda in Verdi's Rigoletto,
letting the birds out of your heart
one
 at
 a
  time.

Whitman loved the Italian opera.
His favorite place for arias was the bathtub,
aggravating both his brother and sister-in-law at mealtime.

My own life connected to his in so many ways;
from height, eye color, occupation and zodiac sign
to having the same house number.
But opera, even the best, often left me to mutter,
along with Whitman's sister-in-law,
"When will it ever stop?"

Opera was more of a joke to me,
like Elmer Fudd belting out "Kill the Wabbit…"
or the champagne glass shattering.

Then just four blocks from Whitman's house,
this contralto soprano sang her death song
and all the jokes stopped.

Something shifted inside me that moonless May night
and I found myself tied to the same mast
as Whitman.

In the morning, trees everywhere
began to fill with singing birds
                         glad to be home.

BUDDHA ORDERS THE LUNCH SPECIAL

A chicken sandwich with fries and a pickle for $2.50.
"You can't beat that," he chuckles.
The barmaid has no idea who she is pouring
a Blue Moon for—in fact no one in the bar does.
Buddha looks more like a renegade
from the 60's—like a disciple of Jerry Garcia's.
Of course if Buddha was younger looking
he might have gotten carded.
Then the barmaid would have known who he was.
She might have asked him to sign the menu
next to the chicken special.
"I thought you were a vegetarian,"
she might have said,
or questioned the sound of one hand clapping.
As it was, when Buddha finishes his sandwich,
she only asks if he wants another beer.
"No thanks," he gives her his full moon smile
and pats his ample stomach.
He leaves a tip that amounts to the price of the sandwich
and gets on his mountain bike to ride home
along the river
through the falling
cherry blossoms.

A CHANCE

I didn't take a chance
and leave my Anti-Thesis on Word Pollution
with a publisher in New York.

I didn't take a chance and really try
at my one and only job interview for
a dance position, even though it would have meant
working with a wonderful Russian dancer named Natasha.

And I didn't take a chance and stay by my father's side
on what would be the last night of his life
at the Mt. Holly hospital. I didn't want to miss
the last bus to Camden.

HAIKU

Father weaves palms
into a cross near the street
where she was shot.

The Muslim man
in black wears a bandolier
of incense.

Over a mountain
of scrap and razor wire
a yellow swallowtail.

TOUCHING HOME

Deep breath—
my friend has ALS.
It's hard to hit the ball when you're blind
so Dave's no Iron Horse.
But he can write poems
that have eyes and

                                                find the gap
                                              in right-center.

Dave sometimes goes long too,
just like Lou
and sends a poem floating over

                    the fence in deep center.

SENRYU

Across the Walt
Whitman Bridge, trucks full
of artificial grass.

Writing haiku
on the back of the tax form
auditing myself.

The five-year-old says
a poem is rhyming letters—
that would save space.

STEPPING

Lamont steps on who cares whose toes.
Jogging to Philly I'd meet him
on the walkway of the Ben Franklin Bridge.
He was on his way to Camden
to pick up his mail. We stood and talked above the river,
and about his daughter, LaMer,
whose name means the sea.

At poetry readings Lamont's words put Jesse Owens
back in the starting blocks. Then he takes me,
who never really knew war,
to smell the napalm in Vietnam.

Another time Lamont brought me
and some other poets inside
Riverfront Prison to do a reading.
I imagine that we inspired another Etheridge Knight
to free his jailed feelings
by committing them to paper.

I admire Lamont's own resolve to publish so many books
and then to actually do it. His last name, Steptoe, is perfect:

Stepping out of the napalm cloud,
Stepping through the prison gate,
Stepping into the runner's blocks
Stepping across creeks and rivers,
Stepping across states and states of mind
Stepping across borders wrapped in barbed wire…
Stepping out to poet's funerals, no matter how far away…

On the Road paying respects to the ones who went before…
No matter how tight money is, Lamont
places a rose on the poet's coffin.

In May he comes to attend the birthday party
of the Good Grey Poet in the backyard
of his Mickel Street home.
He crosses the Delaware from Philadelphia on the ferry
as Walt Whitman himself had done so many times.
The lilacs are not in bloom
so Walt and Lamont stand in front of the rose bush.
Lamont, with Walt's arm on his shoulder,
is still for a few photos
but inside he is busy
stepping toward
the starting line
of another poem.

STILL COUNTING

The deal was a penny for every dandelion
but our yard didn't have enough so I went to Yaskin's
then Stewart's, then Driscoll's. When Momma saw the bucket
full of yellow she had trouble managing her face.
Still, she slowly pulled three dollar bills and some change
out of the dark earth of her purse and I was one rich kid.

Now no dandelions were left to get gray and wise and tell us how
many children we'd have, but by summer's end
there were plenty more. First we'd become the north wind and
blow as hard as we could on the fluff, then we'd count what was left
on the stem. "One, two, three, kids," Judy said,
"and we're helping to make more dandelions."
Good for business, if only Momma would ever hire me again.

Years later an artist using bushel after bushel of dandelions created
a Stonehenge sized wreath on a Scottish hillside.
With my experience I should have applied for the job.

Mother's day is Sunday and my wish
on a head's up penny is for Momma to come down
the crystal stair step into that highland
circle of bright yellow and do a dance of the dandelions for me
and all the children I have taught in Camden.

STELLWAGEN

As the humpback rose right beside the words
"Whale Watcher"
on the port side of our boat,
one big collective breath was held
and then, as the whale dove, let out in disbelief.
The naturalist caught the markings on the tail
and shouted, "it's Samara!"
like she was an old flame that hadn't been fanned in years.
Samara seemed just as excited to see the boat
as she swam under us,
around us and then rested below the bow.

All of a sudden up from beneath the water came
Samara's long white flipper. "She's waving at us,"
a little blond girl exclaimed.
"Samara was a calf here in 2008," the naturalist said,
"her mother was Silla."

Another whale watcher was coming up from behind
and after some more dives and breaches
our captain decided to let that boat
enjoy Samara's playful spirit.

Two men in orange kayaks held fishing poles.
"Are they trying to catch the whale?" someone laughed.

Before we knew it four humpbacks
cut across our bow.
As if it were choreographed, all four whales spouted
at once, baptizing us in a rainbow spray.
Everyone, I think, became an instant believer.
The naturalist could identify three of the four whales,

Jupiter, Storm, and Snowslide,
but he wasn't sure of the other.
"I'll hazard a guess that it might be Hazard.
These four are all young like Samara,"
he went on, "and they're like a bunch of kids
with time on their hands."
"On their flippers," someone corrected him.

We watched the cavorting youngsters until
it was time to head back to Provincetown.
"Fantastic!" a young Frenchman said,
giving me a high five.

The naturalist saved his last bit of whale lore
until we approached the harbor.
He told us that the life span
of a humpback whale can be 80 years.
"Your great grandchildren can come
back here," he said almost tenderly,
"and see these very same whales."

SHE LEFT FOR SIERRA LEONE

Dear Stella,
I called FUN-1313 last night
to take you to the ballet under the stars
but you weren't home, so I went alone.
A boy in a pizza shop said I was a nice man,
so I gave him a quarter to go off and play the machines,
while I went off to see Baryshnikov
and the moon and the city all lit up.

I ate my Italian hoagie at intermission
feeling a little like the guy in the movie,
"Bread and Chocolate,"
who crunched on a hard roll
during a violin recital in the park.
The lady next to me said the sandwich really smelled,
so I ate the rest on the hillside at the next intermission.

I kept my mouth shut during "Push Comes to Shove,"
but at the end I yelled "Bravo!" with my powerful breath.
After that everything kind of glowed innerly,
even going to the bathroom.
I decided to write a book and call it "Camdeners"
like James Joyce's "Dubliners," only more positive.

On the way out I saw a couple kissing on the lawn
and they became a dance.
It's all a dance, isn't it Stella?
No matter what our dance composition teacher says.
It's all a dance, every wave goodbye,
every dash for a train, every fist in the sky,
every check for keys, wallet, or purse.

"It's all a dance," Ram Dass says, "the only dance there is."
He's right, isn't he, Stella? They will know in Africa.
Find out for me. No, no, don't trust the mails.
Sew the answer into the lining of your suitcase.
We don't want this information to get into the wrong hands.
Imagine, everyone a dancer, everything a dance.
Imagine…

SUMMER HAIKU

First hot day of summer.
My cousin dead a year,
wearing his shorts.

Missed all winter,
the clink of ice
in my glass.

On the dune fence
looking out to sea — a pair
of lost glasses.

CODE ORANGE

Does the bridge cop think
I have dynamite strapped to my chest
under the black tank-top?
5-4-3-2-1 **KAPOWIE!!!**
Smoke pours over my shoulder,
fire in the heart
hot mail to heaven,
but it is only a Dali dream.
I am still intact
jogging past the wild sunflowers
and morning glories at the base of the bridge.
The only fire is in the cop's cigarette.
Commuters will get to their computers on time.
There is no need to call all the old ferries
along the river out of retirement,
no need for Churchill or Dunkirk.

Meanwhile, Canadian geese fly low,
echoing the honks above them on the big blue span.
while a cormorant dives straight down 50 feet
looking for fish,
and a man in cut-offs, using a beer can for a reel,
slowly drops his line into the river.

I am lucky to be here.

ON THE BUS TO CAPE MAY

The black dog
on a chain
pacing back and forth
next to the red house.
They were our school colors,
red and black.
They weren't country colors.
They weren't suburban colors either.

When I went west
I bought a print
by an Indian.
The color red
he used for life.
Black, of course,
was for death.

In between
was there a
thin blue road?

BROKEN ARMS

The divorce decree hammered at our hearts
like pickets into the ground of a suburban day.
Curled within were so many false starts
that ended when Daddy's truck pulled away.
He took the pillages of marital war,
the antiques his hands brought back to life.
Yet her wooden arms he could not restore
so he aimed at a new and better wife.
No way to show and tell the tiny flask
once used to catch the salty drippings.
But mother too found another clasp
and song replaced the sound of ripping.
Both parents pressed into a finer second skin
and the walls of war were hammered paper thin.

PUT DOWN DOGS

How come we never talked about my brother, Momma,
who choked on the cord before he even got a name
and one November morning right before Thanksgiving
slipped into the earth above my grandfather's chest?
Was anyone there besides the men with the shovels?
For years, Sandy, my sister
who was seven years younger than me,
wondered what happened to the baby.

How come when you had Sarge, my English Bulldog,
put down at the Vet's, you came home and said,
"There was nothing that could be done," and then told me
they buried Sarge in the Vet's back yard?
Years later I found out vets don't bury dogs
in their backyards.
They all go to mass graves somewhere in the pines.

And now you, Momma, in the nursing home where they pipe
a Jim Croce song down the halls and into your room
where no one mentions the cancer in your lymph nodes,
the inoperable cancer, the fucking Big C.
No one says where you will go, Momma.
My sister and I just tap our feet
To "...Big Bad Leroy Brown,
he's the baddest dude
in the whole damn town..."
and talk about how pretty
the pink dogwood
is out the window.

HAIKU

In the church's corner
beneath the fallen Jesus
a mother rocks her baby.

The list of the sick
my cousin's name gone,
tears on the hymnal.

The little girl picks
a white rose — the petals
cover her black shoes.

STANLEY'S PICTURE

His thin arms carry large buckets,
"Chop wood, carry water"
while his bamboo cane trails behind like a rudder
steering him along the white stone path.
How many buckets has this 100-year-old poet
in the long saffron shirt and brown pants stooped for?
He's seen two Halley's comets scorch the New England sky, but
down here in the garden
away from the whirling cosmic dust ball
he sees juniper, bear grass,
a single wound-up rose bud.
In the foreground in perfect focus
a lace of ferns
descends while
up ahead soft red impatiens
is a little fuzzy for him as well.

Next to the photo
a tape has rewound
and it's almost him.
I press volume up,
"When you write, write down
the previously unspeakable."

Is the unspeakable how I embellished a gay experience
and told the truth about the LSD
and got a letter from a shrink
to get me out of Viet Nam?
Or how my dad came home from the war
and kissed my mother in the kitchen at Ship Bottom?
When I saw them I put my head down
and began to cry.

Or maybe, Stanley Kunitz,
the century old poet-gardener,
means the way I stood up on Herring Cove Beach
with a stone in my hand
and how I rubbed it as I walked by the sea.

How I rubbed until my heart began to pump water
and my arm became the Colorado river
and the stone part of the Grand Canyon
and I wondered how deep
this all would go.

PEACE, BROTHER

The long hair I had shaved off in New Jersey
and had given to my "get a haircut or else" boss
at the Camden Courier-Post
had finally grown back.
No longer reporting on other people's lives,
I woke up in Eddie Suckles' Vancouver high-rise
overlooking the Pacific to The Rascals singing,
"it's a beautiful morning…"
The beauty became its own highway south:
Pollywog Butte, Siskiyou, Gold Beach, Pistol River.

"You've gotta stop at this little laid back fishing village,"
a dark haired woman in Crescent City said, "you'll love it."

Soon I was pulling my green MG Midget off 101
down a gravel road toward a line of fishing boats,
their nets drying in the afternoon sun.
Signs in the window of the no name bar
advertised Olympia and Sierra Nevada beer.
There were no women inside—only tanned Marlboro men
who smelled of salt and mackerel.

"You're not from around here?"
asked a guy in a 49ers T-shirt.
"Not really, actually, I'm looking for work."
"I need a hand," he smiled,
"put your gear on the Susan B. McAllister
at the end of the dock. We'll go out after supper."

I did what he told me and strutted back into the bar,
a marijuana man made good.
"You look happy," a big crew cut guy next to me said.

"I just got a job on the Susan B.
Got my gear on board already."

The guy went apoplectic. "That's my fucking boat, buddy,
and you better get your shit off there right now!"

My sleeping bag and clothes in the car, I, like an idiot,
went back to finish my beer. Just before the fists flew
I ran out to the MG and let my wheels shoot gravel
back at the bar.

I stopped just once to pick wild daisies at Point Reyes
so I could drive across the Golden Gate Bridge
with flowers in my hair.

DEAR MOM,

What did I do to deserve to be raised in Haddonfield
with a little initialed silver pusher to get peas on my spoon?

To deserve growing up across from Hopkins Pond,
where I caught my first sunfish and in the evenings heard
the low moans of mourning doves?

To deserve pink slices of roast beef on my plate
with your corn pudding, every Sunday until the divorce?

To deserve seeing John Wayne on Iwo Jima
and touching Roy Rogers' hat
while he rode Trigger around a ring?

What did my father do to deserve getting the measles
right before D-Day and so survive?

What did I do to deserve friends,
who'd let me mow them down
with a smoking Mattel-burp gun?

To deserve a grandmother with a soft blue velvet couch,
a Pepsi filled ice-box and a cream colored Impala
I could borrow when I turned 17?

To deserve to go to Gettysburg College and live
where all those soldiers died?

To deserve a 1-Y in the draft,
unfit for duty except in a national emergency?
I'll never tell you what I did.

What did my friends, who weren't as smart as me,
or as cowardly, do to deserve Vietnam?

What did my friend, Lanny, do to deserve a Navy father,
who pushed his only son into a war?

What did the wounded Marine do to deserve Lanny,
a medic, risking his own life, to drag him back?

And what has Lanny's mother done to deserve
a locked trunk of letters in a basement
instead of a son.

Love,
Rocky

SURRENDER

Surrender your fort of compassion.

Surrender the feathered down of knowing that softens
the bed for eggs.

Surrender the bleached bone of the whale you carried all the way
back to Camden from Poverty Beach in Cape May.
Surrender the green certainty with which you view
your recyclable life.

Surrender the prom dress, the saddle shoes, and the Buddy Holly
record you were going to get autographed at the
Winter Dance Concert.

Surrender the Sparkle Bitches you found smoking crack at the top
of Apple Pie Hill's fire tower in the Jersey Pine Barrens.
Surrender the sun reflected views of Atlantic City and Philadelphia
in one sweeping gaze.

Surrender the Janis Joplin tickets from the
Electric Factory Concert that you never went to.

Surrender the autographed picture of #36, Robin Roberts, that
you got at the Little League awards dinner at the Hansen House.
Surrender the listening to The Riders of the B-B on the big old
Philco radio with the soft dial glowing in the
early December darkness.

Surrender the license that you forged so you could get served in the
Daytona bar before you were 21.

Surrender the old Rawlings glove you used to catch the liner smashed toward you at third base beside Lake George.

Surrender your hard slap and the sickening howl of your dying dog as he tried to drink the swamp water in the woods
across from your house.

Surrender the toe your uncle said he lost to an alligator on a safari along the Amazon River.

Surrender the toe you lost in the freak work accident and wore preserved around your neck as you motorcycled toward Mt. Everest.

Surrender the American chick you picked up and who freaked out just because you were doing 90 and dug her nails so hard into your ribs that you put her off the cycle to walk back to Nepal. Later you learned she got picked up by 17-year-old machine gun toting Maoists whose eyes were rusty from smoking so much weed.

And surrender your own daughter to the same scenario but try not to think about it.

Surrender your belches and farts and upchucks and surrender your fictitious time with Jack Kerouac on the road and climbing Mt Tamalpais with Gary Snyder.

Surrender the bottle of Jameson, the can of Yuengling,
and the fat doobie.

Surrender The Dharma Bums and the Broadway prostitutes.

Surrender the tattoos, all of them, from "Born to Lose" to the winged woman sitting on the magic mushroom.

Surrender the Gospel. Surrender Buddha's severed concrete head.

Surrender the living flame at Gettysburg that your
first love looked at and started to cry.

Surrender the memory of Abraham Lincoln, the smell of lilacs in
the dooryard, and all the wise words we lost when the Secretary of
State said, "Now he belongs to the ages."
Surrender the one left standing at Little Big Horn,
a horse named Comanche.

Surrender the tied off and cut umbilical cord.

Surrender the memory of a brother who choked on a similar cord.

Don't surrender the woman in Africa named Memory and another
in the same village named Future. When they laugh together near
the well, colorful birds explode out of the trees, and the world is
that much closer

                to being saved.

SHIP BOTTOM

In the sepia picture I hold out
to the pristine sparkle of sun on sea,
three sisters are wearing white
and a fourth, my mother, is wearing a dress
that shows up just a shade darker.
I let the morning sun shimmy over each face in the picture,
lingering over my grandmother in a severe, black dress.
Soon, perhaps, the sisters will actually begin to smile
and do what they loved best, talk.
"Let us stay here," they will plead, beside the sea,
"for we will grow up much too fast."
We will have to crack bottles of champagne
on the bows of huge Navy ships that our father,
Big Colonel, has built in his Camden shipyard.
Before they know it the two older sisters
will be toasting victories in the South Pacific
and downing glass after glass of the bubbly.
Then a cigarette will appear between Bunny's fingers
and a handsome young naval officer will rush to light it.
"Hold us here facing the sea," the sisters cry again.
Let us forget how Big Colonel will teach us to drink
and smoke, so he can see we've become young women.
Let us forget that our mother will focus
on the beatitudes and the cross
and our husbands will drink too much.
Let us forget the lost baby and the lung cancer.
Let us forget the heart failure and the divorces.
We have been grown up far too long,
Let us stay here on the beach.
Let every curling wave wash away something else
and let us sway together.

TRIPPING

To get to Cape Cod the Chinese bus
went through the glowing red confines
of the Holland Tunnel and I saw again
the whale movie that said a small child
could slide through the arteries of a Blue whale.

On the ship outside Provincetown harbor
a troop of teens from a Jewish camp
began to sing old Beatles songs.
And out past the tip of the Cape with its white light house
past the jokes of the guide
"the Pilgrims left because of all the tourists,"
past Herring Cove and the old lifesaving station at Race Point, and
finally out into Stellwagen's Whale Deli
the "Come Together right now..." worked
and I saw the first blow.
Nels, our whale, went in search of Barb
and the two of them sounded together,
rose together and blew together.
Moments later, to everyone's amazement,
the Hebrew children in this new camp
sang "We Shall Overcome" and, then,
the seven stars of Harriet Tubman's drinking gourd
showed bright on the breaching whale's stomach.

Otis Reading's "Dock of the Bay" was the encore
as we walked toward town with our memories stored
on the silver tongues of Nikons and throw-away Fuji's.
Pictures to be enlarged later along with the story
of how the Israelites had once again led us all
out of the wilderness.

THERE ARE NO MOVIE HOUSES LEFT IN CAMDEN

"Guess Who's Coming to Dinner?"
the marquee on the old Stanley Theater asked
and I had ventured in from the suburbs to find out.
I saw Sidney Poitier sit down to eat with the white people
and never dreamed that one day I would be living
a few blocks away, right next to the hospital
where I was born.

Never dreamed that a mother of color,
whose sons broke into my house when I went out,
would invite me to dinner.

Never dreamed that a few months later
there would be a birthday cake
with my name on it.

Never dreamed that one Sunday
this family would take me to church
and rock my Presbyterian up-bringing
to its roots.

"Rock-a my soul in the bosom of Abraham
oh, rock my soul."

Never dreamed that on a
"Take Me Out to the Ballgame" Saturday
I'd be escorted out of Vet Stadium
because the two boys
who had done most of the stealing from me
had poured their Cokes down
on people in the lower level.

Never dreamed I could become so detached
from material things like the clock radio, fan, and typewriter.

Never dreamed a black family
would be calling me, "Uncle Rocky."

Never dreamed that one of the kids
when asked, "How can a white man be your uncle?"
would answer firmly, "He is too our uncle."
Never dreamed that years after that first dinner
I'd be standing before a sea of brown faces,
reading a eulogy I had written for Mom Sumpter.

No, I never dreamed how rich I could become
in the poorest city in America.